St. Basil The

Little Heavenly Heroes for Children

Nokwazi Zimu

Copyright ©Nokwazi Zimu. All rights reserved

Published by Nokwazi Zimu
nzimu@nonomedia.co.za

In terms of the Copyright Act of 1978, no part of this book may be reproduced or transmitted in any form or by any means, electronic or mechanical, including photocopying, recording or by any information storage and retrieval system, without permission in writing from the publisher.

ISBN: 9798854866149

Series Summary

Just like the little children, Saints were also little once, and most of them started doing heroic acts at their youngest age. Some like Padre Pio, fought demons, others, like the Virgin Mary, accepted huge tasks, while others, like Martin de Porres, performed miracles by being in multiple places at once. All these Saints were acting in obedience to God's love and instruction. "Little Heavenly Heroes for Children: Catholic Saints for Kids All Year" is an engaging book series that introduces, inspires and guides young readers about the remarkable and courageous lives of holy Catholic Saints. The Catholic Church holds Saints in high esteem as role models of holiness and devotion to God. Daily reflections inspired by the Saints teach children virtues like compassion, love, and courage. By reading these stories, children can emulate the Saints' faithfulness through lessons, exercises, and practices that apply their timeless wisdom to modern life. Featured Saints from across the globe unite all children of God in growing closer to Him. Each Saint is depicted in full-color images with detailed information about their lives, feast dates, and patronage. These captivating stories of faith and courage make it an ideal gift for children aged 4 and up, especially for first holy communion.

St.Basil the Great Synopsis

This book introduces our little friends to the little heavenly hero called St. Basil the Great. He was kind and clever, from the land of Caesarea, now called Turkey. He loved nature and cared for the sick, even building one of the first hospitals in the world! His family was very special too - his parents, grandmother, and siblings were all saints! When St. Basil inherited wealth from his family, he used it to buy land and build a hospital to help those in need. St. Basil wrote many letters to guide people and defend the Christian faith. His best friend was St. Gregory of Nazianzus, and together, they stood strong for their beliefs. His legacy of kindness and generosity continues to inspire people to help others and be compassionate.

This book belongs to

_____

Feast day: January 2

Birthday: 330 (AD)

Death: 1 January 379 (AD)

Patron of: Hospital administrators, reformers, monks, education, exorcism and liturgists.

Saint Basil was born in a rich and very holy family from Caesarea, in Cappadocia, today known as Turkey. Most of his family members are also Saints - his mom Emmelia and his grandma Macrina the elder, as well as all his siblings, Macrina, Gregory of Nyssa, Peter of Sebastia, and Naucratius.

St. Basil is also known as the protector of the poor, Basil of Caesarea and Father of Eastern Monasticism.

As a young man, Basil received the best education in philosophy, history, rhetoric, astronomy, medicine, and geometry. When he went to study in Athens, Greece Basil became best friends with Saint Gregory, and they remained close for the rest of their lives.

When he finished his studies, Basil went back home to Caesarea. But soon, following his sister's advice, he gave up his career in law and teaching rhetoric to live as a poor monastic instead.

After being baptised, Saint Basil traveled to Palestine, Egypt and Mesopotamia in order to learn more about asceticism or self discipline and monasticism. He gave his wealth to the less fortunate and lived a solitary life for a short while near a place called Neocaesarea.

Although he loved and respected the holiness of a self discipline life, St. Basil didn't like living alone. So he chose to live in a communal religious life.

Within a few years Basil brought together a group of followers of Jesus Christ who shared the same ideas as himself. Amongst these people was his brother, Peter. Together they established a monastic community on his family's land, near Annesi. Soon after that women, including his mom and his sister joined the community. They also committed themselves to the same life of prayer and charity.

Together with his other younger brother, Gregory of Nyssa and his best friend, St. Gregory are collectively known as the Cappadocian Fathers. They started monasteries and set guidelines for community monasticism. During this time Basil started writing about monastic communal life in letters and instructional formats. His work, along with that of the other two Cappadocian Fathers became very influential and respected in the monastic traditions of the Eastern Church.

Their writings and teachings, included the doctrine of the Trinity. They accepted and showed a distinction between the Father, the Son and the Holy Spirit, which was not recognised by the Aryan community of Nicea.

The community denied the divinity of our Lord Jesus Christ and cancelled the value of His sacrifice. But the three Fathers explained it clearly in their writings, and stressed the importance of the unity of the holy trinity as one.

The three Fathers are still respected in both Eastern and Western Churches, today. They are mostly known for their strong support of the Nicene Creed. Experts of education like to say even though the three Fathers had a lot in common, they were still different in some ways. St. Basil was "the man of action", while St. Gregory of Nazianzus was "the great speaker" and his brother, Gregory of Nyssa was "the thinker".

The Nicene Creed

I believe in one God, the Father almighty, maker of heaven and earth, of all things visible and invisible.

I believe in one Lord Jesus Christ, the Only Begotten Son of God, born of the Father before all ages.

God from God, Light from Light, true God from true God, begotten, not made, consubstantial with the Father; through him all things were made.

For us men and for our salvation he came down from heaven,

and by the Holy Spirit was incarnate of the Virgin Mary, and became man.

For our sake he was crucified under Pontius Pilate, he suffered death and was buried, and rose again on the third day in accordance with the Scriptures.

He ascended into heaven and is seated at the right hand of the Father.

He will come again in glory to judge the living and the dead and his kingdom will have no end.

I believe in the Holy Spirit, the Lord, the giver of life, who proceeds from the Father and the Son, who with the Father and the Son is adored and glorified, who has spoken through the prophets.

I believe in one, holy, catholic and apostolic Church.

I confess one Baptism for the forgiveness of sins and I look forward to the resurrection of the dead and the life of the world to come. Amen.

In his position of Bishop of Caesarea, St. Basil served with great love and selflessness. He continued to support the Nicene Creed, and was always very kind to the poor people. Among his kind works of charity, St. Basil ran a soup kitchen, and he distributed food to the poor during a very bad famine. He also donated his personal inheritance to the poor people in his community. St. Basil also worked hard to help thieves and other sinful people change their lives around and dedicate themselves to God.

The three Fathers started hospitals, schools, orphanages and homes for the elderly. All together these institutions made up a small community in a complex called the "Basiliad". It became one of Saint Basil's most notable achievements. The Eastern Roman Emperor Valens, was one of the people who donated land used for building the complex. Most believe the Basiliad was the very first complete hospital to ever exist.

Saint Basil, fought hard against false teachings. He was very brave. He did what many were afraid of doing, like speaking against government officials who were corrupt. He also preached without fear every morning and evening in his own church. He always warned his priests against the temptation of riches and told them that in priesthood, life should not be easy and fun. Saint Basil always took great care when choosing people to follow the life of holy orders.

He continued to write a lot about living and worshiping in the proper Orthodox way. Today he is also known as the author of the Divine Liturgy that has his name, which is celebrated ten times during the year. In Eastern Christianity they also have some religious groups named after him, like The Congregation of St. Basil.

Saint Basil suffered from liver disease and died very poor at the age of 49, on the 1st of January in the year 379. In the Catholic Church his feast day is celebrated on January 2. While in the Eastern Orthodox Church it is celebrated on January 1. One of the important traditions when celebrating St. Basil's Day is to serve vasilopita, which is a sweet bread baked with a coin inside. It is also important to visit friends and relatives, enjoy New Year's with some carol singing, and keeping an extra place at the table for Saint Basil. Feeding the poor, just as Saint Basil did with his soup kitchen, is also very important on. t.

Vasilopita

St Basil Prayers

1st Guidance Prayer

Steer the ship of my life, good Lord, to your quiet harbour, where I can be safe from the storms of sin and conflict. Show me the course I should take.
Renew in me the gift of discernment, so that I can always see the right direction in which I should go.
And give me the strength and the courage to choose the right course, even when the sea is rough and the waves are high, knowing that through enduring hardship and danger, in your name, we shall find comfort and peace.
Amen.

2nd Guidance Prayer

O Lord our God, we beseech you, to ask for the gift we need. Steer the ship of our life to yourself, the quiet harbour of all storm-stressed souls. Show us the course which we are to take. Renew in us the spirit of docility. Let your Spirit curb our fickleness; guide and strengthen us to perform what is for our own good, to keep your commandments and ever to rejoice in your glorious and vivifying presence. Yours is the glory and praise for all eternity. Amen.

Prayer After Communion

We give You thanks, O Lord our God, for the Communion of Your holy, pure, deathless and heavenly mysteries, which you have given for the good, the hallowing, and the healing of our souls and bodies.

Do Thou, O Sovereign of the world, cause this Communion in the Holy Body and blood of Christ to nourish us in unashamed faith, sincere charity, ripe wisdom, health of soul and body, separation from all ills, observance of Your Law, and justification before His awful Judgment Seat.

O Christ our God, the Mystery of Your Providence has been accomplished according to our ability. We have been reminded of Your Death and we have seen a figure of Your Resurrection; we have been filled with Your Infinite Life, and we have tasted Your inexhaustible joy; and we pray to You to make us worthy of these things in the life to come, through the grace of Your Eternal Father and of Your holy, good, and life-giving Spirit, now and forever, eternally.
Amen.

Deeper Sense of Fellowship With All Living Things

O God, grant us a deeper sense of fellowship with all living things, our little brothers and sisters, to whom in common with us You have given this earth as home.

We recall with regret that in the past we have acted high handedly and cruelly in exercising our domain over them thus, the voice of the earth which should have risen to you in song, has turned into a groan of travail.

May we realise that all these creatures also live for themselves and for you, not for us alone. They too love the goodness of life, as we do and serve you better in their way than we do in ours.
Amen.

Nicene Creed

I believe in one God, the Father almighty, maker of heaven and earth, of all things visible and invisible.
I believe in one Lord Jesus Christ, the Only Begotten Son of God, born of the Father before all ages.
God from God, Light from Light, true God from true God,
begotten, not made, consubstantial with the Father; through him all things were made.
For us men and for our salvation he came down from heaven,
and by the Holy Spirit was incarnate of the Virgin Mary, and became man.
For our sake he was crucified under Pontius Pilate, he suffered death and was buried, and rose again on the third day in accordance with the Scriptures.
He ascended into heaven
and is seated at the right hand of the Father.
He will come again in glory to judge the living and the dead and his kingdom will have no end.
I believe in the Holy Spirit, the Lord, the giver of life, who proceeds from the Father and the Son, who with the Father and the Son is adored and glorified, who has spoken through the prophets.
I believe in one, holy, catholic and apostolic Church.
I confess one Baptism for the forgiveness of sins and I look forward to the resurrection of the dead and the life of the world to come. Amen.

ST. BASIL THE GREAT WORD SEARCH

```
Y R E T S E N O M H Z N J G X
S L Z C R Z S L V K T C E T P
A D U V C M O J A D M A N T K
I G E U D J U E S Q W B A T S
N O Q E B A I H I L U E H N E
T K V A R V E T L T R B V U D
W Q S L C C T J O G A S O W G
A I Z I B D P Z P S Z P B A N
L E H T E N E C I N I I X U Q
B P R A X A F L T Q L F M G L
Z J M A I C I C A F S L V P B
C M L H S A G N F S B B K N P
D T M P D E Q S O Y N P P L D
A Y Z L E R A W G R E G O R Y
U U D A P Q L C C Q D G M S A
```

- BASILIAD
- BASIL
- GREGORY
- CAESAREA
- MONESTERY
- SAINT
- GREAT
- THE
- VASILOPITA
- CREED
- NICENE

Match the picture to the name

The Basiliad

Nicene Creed

Church

St. Basil

Vasilopita

Get the kids to the giant Vasilopita

Quiz for clever boys and girls

What year was St. Basil born?

What country does he come from?

Who is his best friend?

What was St. Basil's sister's name?

What did St. Basil do to his wealth?

What was the community St. Basil built with his friend Gregory and brother Gregory?

THE END

www.ingramcontent.com/pod-product-compliance
Ingram Content Group UK Ltd.
Pitfield, Milton Keynes, MK11 3LW, UK
UKHW051318190125
4173UKWH00032B/292